This Book Belongs To

First Name ____________________

Last Name ____________________